RIPARIAN AREA MANAGEMENT

Observing Physical and Biological Change
Through Historical Photographs

by

Earl Hindley

Bureau of Land Management
Utah State Office

Technical Reference 1737-13
1996

U.S. Department of the Interior
Bureau of Land Management
National Applied Resource Sciences Center
P.O. Box 25047
Denver, CO 80225-0047

Acknowledgements

The author wishes to acknowledge the assistance of Jerry Sintz, whose knowledge of cameras, film, and photographic techniques was most helpful in the development of this document.

Table of Contents

Observing Physical and Biological Change Through Historical Photographs

I. Introduction

The recent emphasis on ecosystem management in the Bureau of Land Management (BLM) and other Federal agencies has raised significant issues, such as how to define terms, measure ecosystem health, and project what conditions can be attained by applying various land use management strategies. One of the most debated and contested issues revolves around landscape conditions prior to or during early Anglo settlement and development of the West. There is a wide divergence of opinion about vegetation and stream channel conditions that preceded current conditions.

Historic photographs can portray the character of landscapes as they were in the latter 1800's and early 1900's. Retaking photos from the same location can provide comparisons from which vegetation (Rogers, 1982) and stream channel changes (Graf, 1978) can be objectively described. Such visual comparisons are also useful in depicting the dynamic nature and resiliency of ecosystems, and in dispelling some of the myths that exist regarding historic conditions and the circumstances that caused them.

II. Purpose

BLM has published several technical references to aid its field personnel in managing the 269 million acres of public lands and resources for which it is responsible. Many of these technical references emphasize the need to collect and analyze historic information in order to better assess the potential of ecological sites. The purpose of this technical reference is to provide resource specialists with the basic information, concepts, and procedures associated with using historical photographs to analyze changes that have occurred on specific ecological sites in relationship to possible change agents.

This document supplements technical references 1737-7, *Procedures for Ecological Site Inventory—with Special Reference to Riparian-Wetland Sites* (Leonard et al., 1992); 1737-9, *Process for Assessing Proper Functioning Condition* (Prichard et al., 1993); 1737-10, *The Use of Aerial Photography to Manage Riparian-Wetland Areas* (Clemmer, 1994); and 1737-11, *Process for Assessing Proper Functioning Condition for Lentic Riparian-Wetland Areas* (Prichard et al., 1994).

III. Uses and Limitations

A series of repeated photos can be an excellent tool for quantifying the rate, nature, and direction of change of the vegetation or stream channel at an ecological site (Rogers et al., 1984). It also provides a common base and creates a forum for analyzing factors in and causes of observed changes. In addition, it provides a compelling look at historic conditions and trends. However, there are certain limitations to using historic photos for these purposes.

One major limitation to using historic photos for comparison is that often the photographer was interested in showcasing something different than that which is to be analyzed. For example, early photos taken by geologists often show geologic formations or mineral deposits, with perhaps a slight glimpse of surrounding vegetation or drainage patterns. Photos taken by cadastral surveyors most likely show the topography along the survey line, with little regard for surrounding vegetation or soil surface conditions. Another common situation is that the once-open landscapes captured in historic photos are now often cluttered with cultivated fields, buildings, parking lots, or freeways. However, such limitations can also prove to be advantageous because the photographs can be considered a random scene that cannot be construed to be a biased representation of changes which have or have not occurred.

The inherent potential for biases in selecting photos to be retaken and analyzed is another potential limitation. Again, the original photographers possessed their own reasons for taking each photo. If they chose to take a series of photos depicting south-facing slopes or areas that were especially denuded, then repeating the photos will not depict the true nature of any specific area as a whole. Therefore, the most effective comparisons will be those where a wide variety of photos from as many photographers as possible can be used. When a variety of historic photos are available, selection should not be limited to only those that depict the desired conditions. This, of course, will result in inaccurate conclusions and cast doubt on the credibility of the analysis.

Difficulty in duplicating the photo equipment, camera type, film, lens angle, and focal length of the original photo for the retake can also limit the usefulness of historic photos. A wide variety of equipment has been used over the last 100 years. The time of year; time of day; presence, absence, or angle of sunlight; camera angle; and even framing of the image should be considered in selecting and retaking photos because they can all influence the results of the comparative analysis. The quality of the original negative may also be a factor.

Finally, vegetation species can be difficult to identify from historic photos. However, vegetation classes can be readily determined; thus, relative vegetation compositions and densities can be identified. Relative widths, depths, and angles of stream channel cuts also can be determined through photo comparisons.

IV. Method

The use of repeat photography is not a new concept, and there are many fine examples of such work available. A few notable publications include a photographic study of vegetation changes in southern Wyoming from 1870 to 1986 (Johnson, 1987), a photographic history of vegetation change in the Great Basin (Rogers, 1982), an extensive analysis of channel changes in Kanab Creek in Utah and Arizona (Webb et al., 1991), and a repeat photography project which includes 120 photo pairs from six Western States (Klett et al., 1984). Graf (1978) used repeat photography techniques to establish a timetable for tamarisk invasion and determine the resulting fluvial changes on the lower Green River in Utah. Rogers et al. (1984) completed a comprehensive bibliography of repeat photography publications from around the United States and several foreign countries.

Photographing the same scene as a photographic pioneer can provide a sense of exhilaration—there is a certain excitement to standing on the exact spot where William Henry Jackson, John K. Hillers, or Timothy H. O'Sullivan stood over 100 years ago. But more importantly, when done properly, significant understanding can result from the effort. The following process will help ensure that the replication of a historic photo is accurate and the results of the photo comparison are valid.

A. Research Existing Photos

Old photos can be found literally anywhere. Useful historic photos are found in private collections, museums, libraries, universities, historical societies, and many other locations. However, Rogers (1982) notes that there is often little correlation between the archival location of the photograph and the location where it was taken. Although it is a good idea to start researching possibilities close to the geographic area of interest, applicable photos may be found in unlikely places. Rogers (1982) points out that the University of Arizona Herbarium has "thousands" of negatives, many of which were taken in the Bonneville Basin.

The single most important source for research on BLM-administered lands is the U.S. Geological Survey photo library in Denver, Colorado. This well-documented and cataloged collection contains thousands of old photos and negatives from throughout the West and other sections of the nation. The material dates from the 1860's to the present.

Rogers et al. (1984) provide a partial listing of sources for historic photos, some of which are listed in Table 1. However, local sources, such as private collections, local historical entities, and BLM files, should not be overlooked. In fact, BLM has many excellent photos dating from the early days of the Grazing Service.

Table 1. Partial list of sources for historic photographs.

American Division of Natural History Photography Library 79 Street, Central Park West New York, NY 10024-5192	Museum of Natural History Smithsonian Institution 10th Constitution Ave N.W. Washington, DC 20560
Brigham Young University Archives and Manuscripts 5030 HBLL Provo, UT 84602-6877	Photo Archives Museum of New Mexico P.O. Box 2087 Santa Fe, NM 87504-2087
Colorado Historical Society Colorado Heritage Center 1300 Broadway Street Denver, CO 80203	Photographic Archives Bancroft Library University of California Berkley, CA 94720-6000
LDS Church Archives 50 East North Temple Salt Lake City, UT 84150	Special Collections Library Northern Arizona University Flagstaff, AZ 86011
Library of Congress Prints and Photographs Section 1st Street Independence Ave. S.E. Washington, DC 20540	Special Collections and Archives Merrill Library Utah State University Logan, UT 84322-3000
Life Picture Service Time Life Building Rockefeller Center 1271 6th Ave New York, NY 10020	The National Geographic Society 17th and M Streets N.W. Washington, DC 20036
Marriot Library Special Collections University of Utah Salt Lake City, UT 84112	Utah State Historical Society 300 Rio Grande Salt Lake City, UT 84101

In addition, there are several excellent sources for aerial photos, dating from the late 1920's, which can also serve vital needs (Table 2).

Table 2. Partial list of sources for historic aerial photographs.

Agricultural Stabilization and Conservation Service 222 West 2300 South P.O. Box 30010 Salt Lake City, UT 84130-0010
National Archives 8601 Adelphi Road College Park, MD 20740-6001
EROS Data Center U.S. Geological Survey Sioux Falls, SD 57198

B. Locate The Original Photopoint

The philosophy of repeat photography is to recreate, as nearly as possible, the same conditions under which the original scene was photographed. The most important aspect of recreating a photo is to find the photopoint, the exact point from which the original photo was taken, and retaking the photo from the same location. Finding the original location can sometimes be quite easy, or it can be very difficult. Often the original scene is familiar to field personnel, or the photograph contains enough background so that, with a little ground searching, the location can successfully be found. Regardless, it often takes considerable time to replicate the scene. If there are identifiable features such as rocks, trees, etc., in the immediate foreground, replication is relatively simple (refer to Appendix A, photo comparisons 1 and 2). On the other hand, if the scene is a wide expanse with little foreground, it becomes more difficult to occupy the original photopoint. Relative distances between identifiable objects or topographical features on the original photo should be matched both vertically and horizontally. This can be accomplished through "trial and error," by moving parallel to, closer to, or farther from the object in the center of the original photo. A Polaroid[1] camera and instant film should be considered for the process of checking the location, otherwise two or more field trips may be required to duplicate the image. In some cases, the exact location may not be critical, and approximations may be all that is necessary (refer to Appendix A, photo comparison 5). Rogers et al. (1984) and Veatch (1969) report that valid comparisons can be made even when repeat photographs do not match exactly. These photos may provide intermediate photos that are useful for demonstrating trends. Often BLM files contain photos which may not exactly duplicate the scene, but are close enough to illustrate changes.

---

[1] Any use of trade, product, or firm names in this publication is for descriptive purposes only, and does not imply endorsement by the U.S. Government.

C. Replicate the Conditions

When retaking a photo, it is best to take it at the same time of year and the same time of day as the original photo. Unfortunately, early photographers rarely recorded the exact date and time of day their image was made. Images can be misleading if similar lighting with resulting shadowing is not replicated. Likewise, if vegetative growth stages are not approximately the same, the resulting analysis will be erroneous. Obviously, if an original photograph of a riparian habitat was taken in the early spring, and was retaken in the summer, the growth stages of existing riparian vegetation in the retake will tend to slant the analysis. This of course, is also true if the new image is taken either right after an area has had a rest from grazing or after a grazing cycle has just been completed. Varying sun angles and elevations result in different shadows, which change specific qualities of the image. For example, long shadows give the appearance of more vegetation density in a scene. Such differences will likely occur in most efforts to repeat photos, and should be accounted for in the resulting analysis in order to ensure its credibility.

D. Replicate the Equipment

Because most photographers did not record the camera format or focal length of the lens they used, it may be impossible to determine the appropriate equipment to use before going to the field to rephotograph a site. In their 1987 study, Stephens and Shoemaker (1987) report that early photographers of the Colorado River used extremely wide-angle lenses in many instances, and they found that their backup camera with a 47-mm lens was ultimately the most suitable for rephotographing the scenes. This equipment provided a 2 1/4- by 3 1/4-inch format, which is roughly equivalent to a 22-mm lens on a 35-mm camera. When the finished prints were made, they were cropped to match the image in the historical photo.

Rogers et al. (1984) indicate that it is more accurate to use a lens with a greater angle of view (e.g., wide-angle lens) than to try to match the focal length of the original camera lens. Regardless of the lens used, if the photograph is taken from the same lens position, the photographs will always match if both are printed and cropped to the same size (Rogers et al., 1984).

Usually, modern cameras with wide-angle zoom lenses will allow the photographer retaking the photo to match the original scene without having to return to the site a second time. A camera equipped with a 24- to 50-mm zoom lens (84 to 46 degrees) will usually suffice. Occasionally, some original photographs were made with lenses that encompassed 120 to 180 degrees or more. In those cases, a special wide-view camera will be required, or the available equipment will have to be used with a tripod. The tripod head will need to be leveled and a sequence of overlapping photographs taken. Then the final prints should be cropped to effect proper edge matches. This minimizes any lens distortions at the edges of the photograph, errors in the position of the camera lens, and differences in angle of view between the old and new photos.

A good fine-grained, black-and-white film, such as Kodak T-Max 100 or Plus-X, can be used in 35-mm photography. Faster film, such as Kodak T-Max 400 or Tri-X, may be used for medium or large formats if the extra film speed is necessary. Prints up to 8 by 10 inches from these films provide adequate resolution for comparison with old photographs. Filters usually are not necessary with modern black-and-white films because they are sensitive to all colors. A medium yellow filter may be used, but stronger filters, such as orange or red, alter tonal values to the point that comparison of vegetation or other features may be difficult. Color film should not be used if the original photo is black and white because direct comparisons are more difficult and can be misleading.

Bracketing exposures in increments of one f-stop is recommended for black-and-white film. For example, exposing one frame at the indicated meter reading (f-16), a second at one full stop above the indicated meter reading (f-22), and a third at one full stop below the indicated meter reading (f-11), will guarantee a suitable print and an extra negative in case of loss or damage.

Carrying a second 35-mm camera loaded with a medium-speed (ISO 50-100) color transparency film and a 24- to 50-mm or 28- to 50-mm zoom lens provides a color slide of the scene being rephotographed. Bracketing exposures in one-half-stop increments is recommended to ensure that a slide with the detail needed for projection purposes or for making prints is obtained.

Excellent color slides have been made by copying black-and-white prints with a macrolens. The slides of the before and after photos can be loaded into two slide projectors side by side, and the comparisons can be shown at meetings or briefings.

E. Establish a Permanent Record

A permanent record should be established that contains pertinent information about the photo to be retaken. Figure 1 is a sample field data sheet showing the types of information to be included. Data sheets can be altered or expanded to suit individual needs.

Recording the location of the exact photopoint is critical for future replications of an image. There are several steps which will help ensure that the photopoint can be relocated:

- The photopoint should be accurately marked on a U.S. Geological Survey (USGS) 7.5-minute quadrangle and aerial photo, if available. A location from a Global Positioning System would also be helpful.

- As a minimum, the legal description, to the nearest 40 acres, should be noted on the field data sheet, along with a narrative describing the general location.

- One or more photos of the site should be taken from nearby vantage points so that future photographers can see the exact location. Permanent features that are readily identifiable should be included in these reference photos.

- A small iron stake should be driven and a small rock cairn built directly below the camera lens.

PHOTOGRAPHY FIELD DATA

Photo Number: _____

Location: _____

View Direction: _____

General Description: _____

_____

Original Photo	**Duplicate Photo**
Date: _____	Date: _____
Time of Day: _____	Time of Day: _____
Photographer: _____	Photographer: _____
Photo Source: _____	Camera Information: _____
_____	_____
Vegetation:	Vegetation:
Comments:	Comments:

Figure 1. Sample field data sheet.

8

- An iron fence post should be located several yards from the site and its location to the photopoint referenced on the field data sheet.

All of the above information should be included in the permanent record. In some instances it will be necessary to move the photopoint, because vegetation or other obstacles now obscure the scene. In such cases, it will be critical to explain the reasons for the move and describe the new location in relationship to the original camera location. It is also suggested that a photo be taken from the original location to illustrate the changes that have occurred.

Each photo taken should be accompanied by basic information, including the date, time of day, and photographer. Specific information regarding view angle, exposure, film type, filters used, camera height, etc., should also be included on the field data sheet. In addition, lighting and atmospheric conditions at the time the photo is retaken should be noted, as such information may be helpful during comparison and analysis.

All relevant vegetation and physical conditions should be recorded while at the site. Vegetation information could include composition and densities, as well as the species list. It is important to include any information that could assist in interpreting changes that have or have not occurred. Any people, horses, or permanent features visible in the scenes should also be noted, as they may be helpful in determining approximate scales.

V. Analysis

The objective of this process is to analyze vegetation and physical changes within a scene by comparing historic and recent photos and relating the information to the potential and capability of specific sites. However, the significance attached to the comparison should not be more than can be reasonably supported. For example, photographs taken in the late 1800's or early 1900's most likely will not illustrate pre-Anglo settlement conditions in the Western United States. The resulting analysis must focus on the changes that have occurred in the scene since the original photo was taken and cannot be used to approximate a so-called "pristine" state unless accompanying documentation will support such a declaration. Mason (1963) found that historical records are often detailed enough to allow resource specialists to determine the relative vegetative composition of specific ecological sites. Invaluable data can be found in records such as climatic reports, hydrographs, periodicals, newspaper accounts, journals, cadastral survey notes, archaeological study reports (pollen and vegetative remains), and earlier research efforts. Thus, visual comparisons can and should be augmented and supported by any available information.

Appendix A provides some example comparisons of historic and recent photos and illustrates the kinds of information that can typically be obtained from them. This information, when coupled with information from other historical records, provides a more complete picture of previous conditions at a site.

Appendix A: Photo Comparisons

1. Virgin River Near Grafton, Utah

These photos were taken looking southeast toward the town of Grafton, near the mouth of Coal Pits Wash (NW¼ NW¼ sec. 3, T. 41 S., R. 11 W.). The original photo (1a) was taken in the summer of 1906 (Lee, USGS). It was retaken (1b) in April 1993 (Hindley, BLM). Note the white rock in the lower left foreground for orientation.

The original photo shows a wide and shallow channel with little vegetation present along the banks. The vegetation in the foreground appears to be little rabbitbrush and cholla. The retake shows a much more developed, narrow channel with vegetated banks and a defined, vegetated, flood plain. The riparian vegetation includes cotton-wood, Russian olive, coyote willow, seepwillow, rush species, and a few scattered tamarisk.

A third photograph (1c), taken from almost the same location in January 1941 (Grant, BLM), shows that few changes in the channel or vegetative conditions occurred between 1906 and 1941. The 1941 image does show some willow on the far bank, as well as some agricultural development on the developing lateral bar.

Photo 1a.

Photo 1b.

Photo 1c.

2. Virgin River Near St. George, Utah

The point from which these photos were taken is a small bluff looking northwest into St. George, Utah (SW¼ SE¼ sec. 33, T. 42 S., R. 15 W). The Utah State Historical Society owns the original photograph (2a), which was taken sometime in the 1920's. The photographer is unknown. The photo was retaken (2b) in June 1993 (Hindley, BLM).

A wide, shallow, braided channel is clearly visible in the original photo. The river is obviously carrying more sediment than the system can flush. The vegetation along the banks appears to be willow species, possibly seepwillow or arrowweed. In 1870, Gorlinski conducted the cadastral survey in this township. When running the north/south line between sections 32 and 33, he measured the channel width at 1,172 feet. There was no road on the south bank of the river in 1870. Construction of the road evidently constricted the channel between the 1870 survey and the 1920's photo.

The 1993 image shows a much more distinct, narrower, and deeper channel. The flood plains are heavily vegetated. However, the point bar has remained essentially unvegetated for 70 years. Plant species on the first (lower) terrace consist of coyote willow, seepwillow, cattail, common reed, rush species, and sparse cottonwood and tamarisk seedlings. The second terrace supports coyote willow, Gooding willow, seepwillow, arrowweed, young cottonwood trees, common reed, Bermuda grass, and some tamarisk. The third or highest terrace is dominated by dense tamarisk.

3. Virgin River Near St. George, Utah

These aerial photos show a reach of the Virgin River (sec. 16, T. 42 S., R. 14 W). The original photo (3a) was taken on October 5, 1952. It was retaken (3b) on June 24, 1993.

These photos, in conjunction with early cadastral survey field notes and plats, give a solid indication as to how and why the river channel migrated back and forth across its flood plain due to land use practices at this particular location. As Mayhew Dalley surveyed this township in 1899, he noted that local farmers had constructed a diversion dam across the Virgin River (SW¼ NE¼ sec. 16) for the purpose of irrigating their fields via a ditch that they had constructed on the west side of the valley (refer to the cadastral survey plat, Figure 2). The 1952 aerial photograph shows the entire Virgin River had altered its course to follow the irrigation ditch. On a 1976 USGS 7.5-minute quadrangle (not shown), the river had partially reverted to its 1899 location on the east side of the valley, a migration of over 1,000 feet.

Cultural resource investigations and journals from early explorers and settlers, as well as cadastral survey field notes, give an indication of the historic vegetative and channel conditions along the river. Settlers' written descriptions, newspaper articles, and more recently, hydrograph and precipitation records provide accounts of flood and drought events. Previous research regarding long-range channel evolution processes in similar locations, along with the photo record (including comparisons 1, 2, and 3), can be analyzed to give a much clearer understanding of the Virgin River as it now exists.

Photo 2a.

Photo 2b.

14

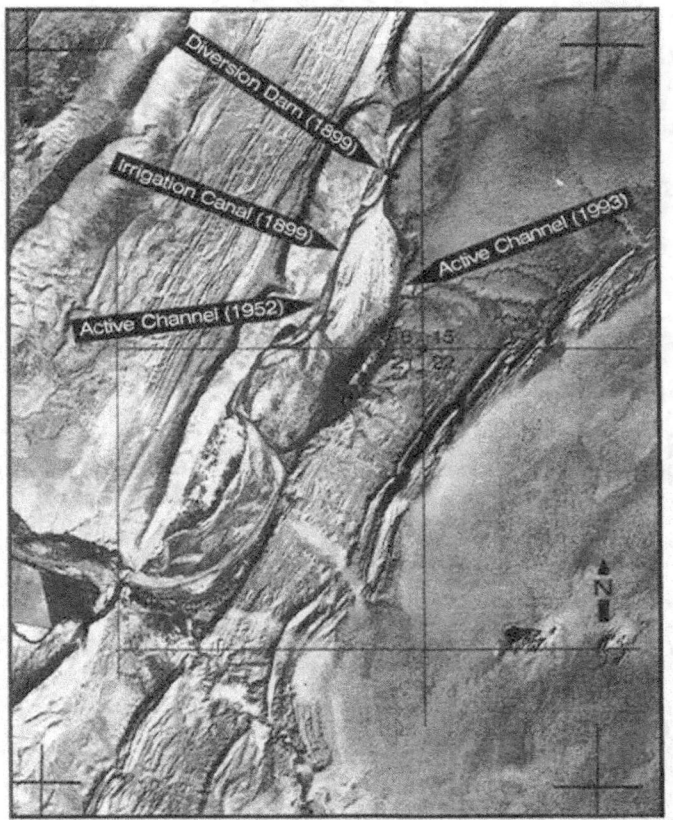

Photo 3a.

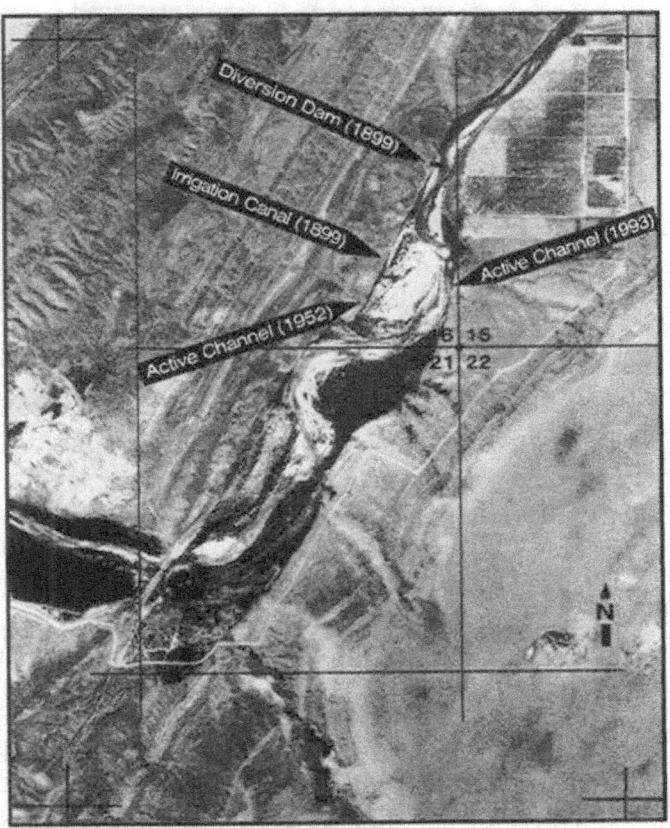

Photo 3b.

15

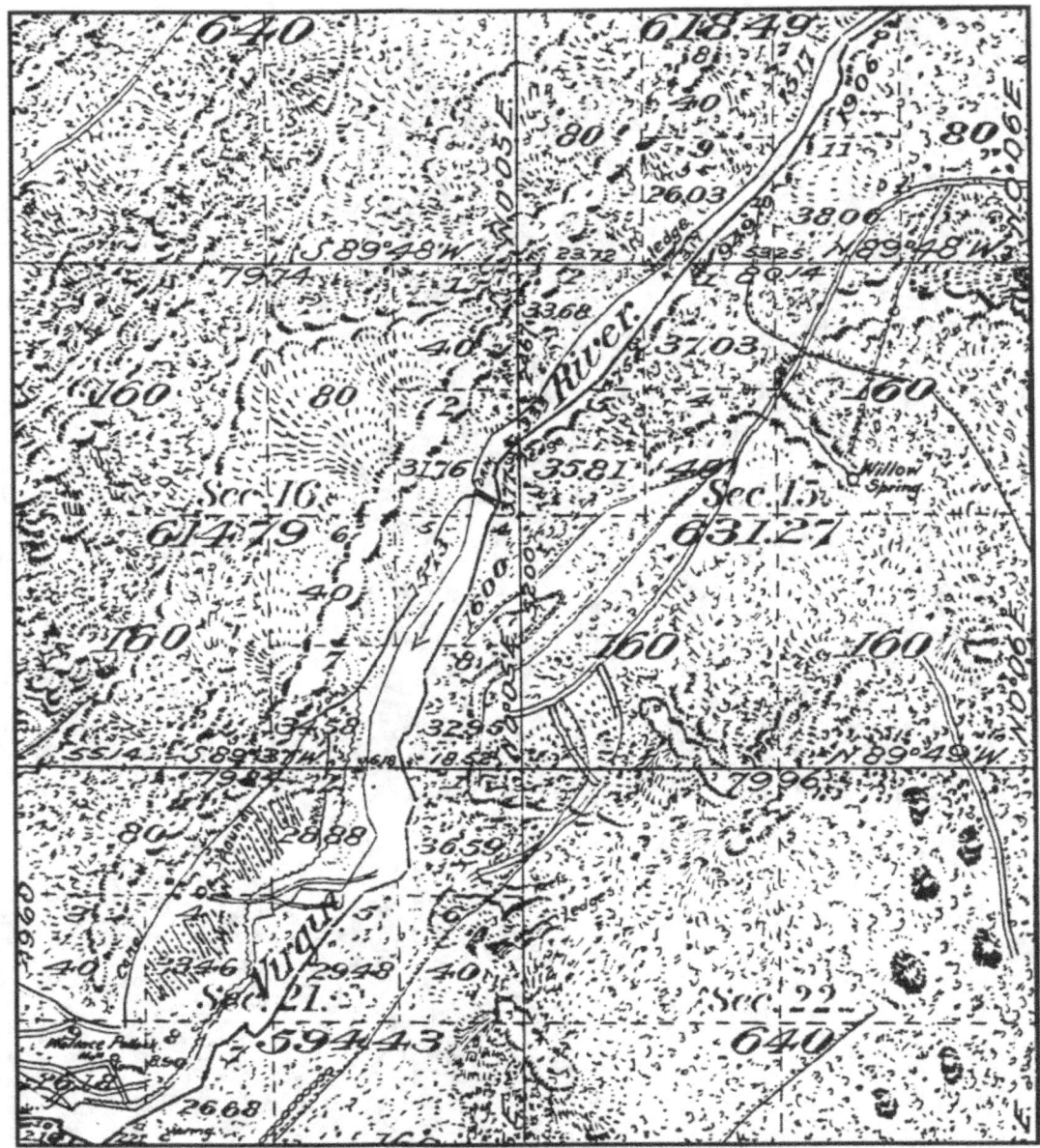

Figure 2. Cadastral survey plat of T. 42 S., R. 14 W. completed by Mayhew H. Dalley in June 1899.

From the available historic record (not all of which is presented in these three comparisons), it is evident that the Virgin River has supported a classic southwestern riparian vegetation association consisting of trees, such as cottonwood, black willow, and ash, and small willows, bulrush, rush, and sedges. However, the record is not clear as to just how dense or extensive these riparian communities were. In general, it appears that the upper river (above the Virgin River Gorge) had "extensive" cottonwood stands, while cottonwoods along the lower river were most likely associated with springs (Linhart, 1993).

The record also indicates that the Virgin River, along with other rivers and streams in the Southwestern United States, is continually undergoing cyclic aggrading-degrading processes that result in major channel and vegetative changes. The most recent degrading event in the late 1800's and early 1900's seems to have been exacerbated by land use and livestock grazing practices (Gregory, 1950).

Photographic evidence shows that the Virgin River has made major evolutionary progress in the past 30-40 years toward a much more productive state, and that the tamarisk invasion has been both a deterrent and a benefit to stabilization of the channel.

USGS hydrograph records taken at Virgin, Utah, show peak river flows from 1910 through 1986, with the exception of a 7-year data gap from 1972 to 1978 (Figure 3). These records show that from 1910 to 1941 (the date of photo 1c), there were 10 years where peak flows exceeded 5,000 cubic feet per second (cfs) and 5 years where peak flows exceeded 10,000 cfs. From 1942 to 1986, excluding the 7-year gap, flows in 12 years exceeded 5,000 cfs and during 5 of those years, flows exceeded 10,000 cfs. Four of the five highest peak flows, 13,000 cfs or above, occurred from 1953 to 1969; the other occurred prior to 1941. The record high flow of 22,800 cfs occurred in December 1967. This record shows that peak flows from 1942 to 1986 have been equal to or greater than those occurring from 1910 to 1941.

If past land use and grazing practices are to be cited for intensifying the stream channel degradation that occurred near the turn of the century, then revisions made in such management, starting in the late 1950's and early 1960's, should be credited for a portion of the channel aggradation made in the last half of this century. Webb et al. (1991) state, for Kanab Creek, a drainage adjacent to the Virgin River, "The advent of current Grazing Allotments in 1963-64 resulted in changes of seasonality of grazing that may have had the largest effect on improving range conditions."

Dynamic channel and river adjustments have undoubtedly impacted fish and wildlife species that inhabit the river and riparian zones adjacent to the river. These impacts, along with cause and effect relationships, warrant further investigation.

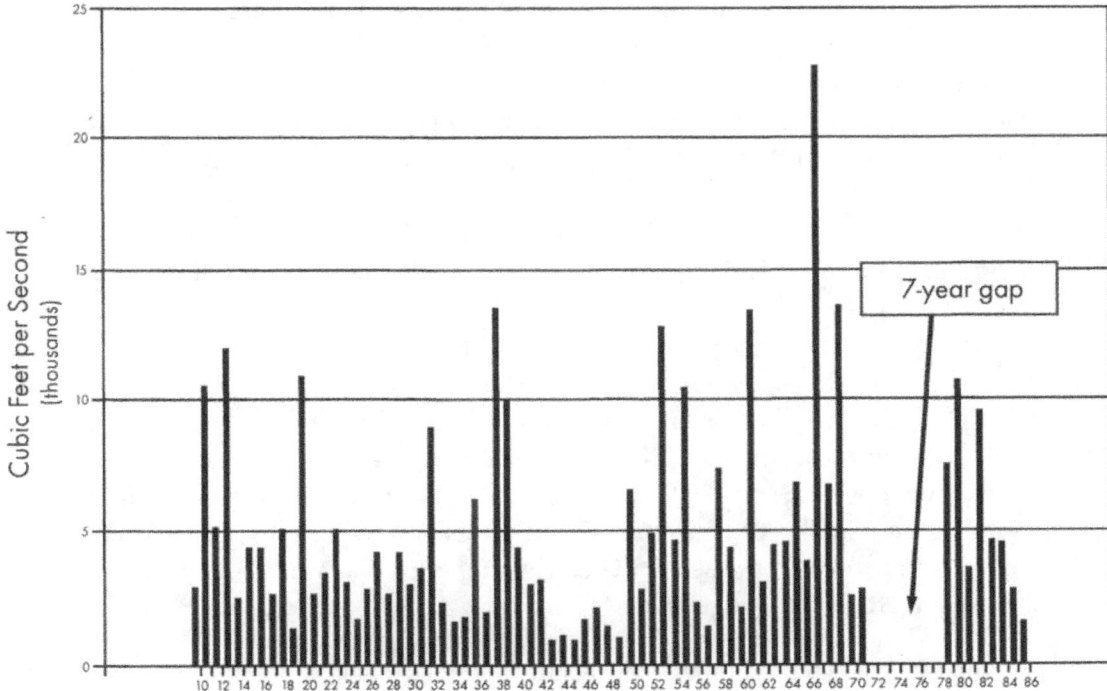

Figure 3. Virgin River peak discharge at Virgin, Utah from 1910 to 1988.

4. Kanab Creek Near Kanab, Utah

These photos demonstrate the historical changes that have occurred over 54 years along Kanab Creek, a deeply incised stream channel. The original photo (4a) was taken in 1939 (Gregory, USGS). The photo was retaken (4b) in April 1993 (Hindley, BLM). Remarkable improvements, such as channel narrowing and establishment of dense riparian vegetation, including cottonwood, willow, black willow, cattail, common reed, sedges, and rush species, are obvious. Tamarisk plants occupy a midlevel terrace, but are being replaced by native riparian species on the lower terrace adjacent to the active channel. Previous raw, active cutbanks have evolved into a relatively stable condition. Other than the increase of rabbitbrush and sagebrush on the cutbanks, little change is apparent in the uplands. Some of the same pinyon/juniper plants are still visible. Conditions at the mouth of Tiny Canyon (right center of photos) have improved with the recent establishment of cottonwood trees in the riparian zone. An intermediate photograph (not shown), taken at the same location in 1984 (Webb et al., 1991), does not show cottonwoods in the mouth of Tiny Canyon.

5. Escalante River Near Escalante, Utah

Dramatic improvement in channel and riparian vegetation conditions along the Escalante River is apparent from these photos. They were taken approximately 13 miles east of Escalante, Utah at the Boynton's Point overlook (SW¼ SW¼ sec. 12, T. 35 S., R. 4 E). The original photo (5a) was taken about 1950 (Woodbury, University of Utah Special Collections). It was retaken (5b) in May 1995 (Hindley, BLM).

Channel conditions in the 1950 image show a wide, shallow, braided stream with a few widely scattered cottonwood trees. The channel, now a single stem, is much narrower and deeper. Calf Creek, which enters the Escalante River in the left center of the photographs, also exhibits a marked improvement. Existing vegetation includes cottonwood, boxelder, willow, sedge, rush, and cattail, with a few Russian olive and tamarisk plants. In the early 1960's, the livestock grazing system was changed from a season-long (fall through spring) to a late fall/early winter period of use.

This is an example where the exact location need not be duplicated because of the readily identifiable topographic markers from which an analysis can be made.

6. San Rafael River Near Green River, Utah

The photos of the San Rafael were taken in Emery County approximately 15 river miles south of Interstate 70 (SE¼ NE¼ sec. 1, T. 24 S., R. 14 E.). The view is downstream on a private parcel of land, which remains unfenced from surrounding BLM-administered land. An ephemeral drainage, Cottonwood Wash, enters the San Rafael at the right center of the scene. The original photo (6a) was taken around 1917 (Emery, USGS). It was retaken (6b) on June 8, 1994 (Hindley, BLM).

Comparison of the two photos reveals that the previously barren point bar has stabilized and expanded toward the right bank. The active channel has narrowed and increased in depth. The mouth of Cottonwood Wash now supports numerous cottonwood

18

Photo 4a.

Photo 4b.

19

Photo 5a.

Photo 5b.

Photo 6a.

Photo 6b.

seedlings and five to six 6-year old cottonwood poles. No young cottonwood plants appear in the 1917 image. However, there are apparently some rush or bulrush plants at the mouth of Cottonwood Wash in 1917. The 1994 photo shows some active bank cutting on the outside bend.

Vegetation on the low terrace in the 1994 photo (left bank) consists of cottonwood seedlings, coyote willow, common reed, yellow sweet clover, rabbitbrush, and tamarisk plants. Rush species and bulrush inhabit the area immediately adjacent to the active channel. Tamarisk plants account for about 30-35 percent of the composition on the low terrace. The composition and density of tamarisk plants increases with the distance and elevation from the active channel. The higher terrace, visible on the right bank, is occupied by a dense stand of mature tamarisk (foreground) and a cottonwood gallery mixed with tamarisk and rabbitbrush plants (background). In addition, blowing sand activity has significantly decreased in the 77 years between photographs.

7. Coal Bed Ruins Near Blanding, Utah

The view in these photos is to the south across ancient Anasazi ruins at the confluence of Coal Bed Creek, entering from the left of the scene, and Montezuma Creek, at the right (SE¼ NE¼ sec. 2, T. 37 S., R. 24 E.). The original photo (7a) was taken in 1875 (Jackson, USGS). It was retaken (7b) on August 3, 1994 (Hindley, BLM).

The ruin site is formed by a rocky ridge, which immediately drops to a flood plain terrace. The terrace was evidently farmed by the inhabitants of the area. It is readily apparent that major changes have occurred at this site in the 119 years between photographs.

Vegetation on the flood plain in the 1875 image is difficult to identify. What appear to be willow plants are found in the lower left of the scene, and willow and cottonwood trees are found along Montezuma Creek to the right. Other flood plain vegetation is unknown, but may consist of common reed, willow, cattail, or even wild rye. Corn stalks may be visible in the open space located in the right center portion of the 1875 image.

It is clearly evident that the flood plain terrace of 1875 has been mostly lost with downcutting and entrenchment of both Coal Bed Creek and Montezuma Creek. With the available record, it is not possible to tell exactly when the change occurred. However, research conducted at other sites in southern Utah and northern Arizona (Gregory, 1950; Webb et al., 1991) indicates that major stream degradations occurred in this region beginning in the 1870's and 1880's. The 1994 photo clearly shows that the two channels now support several age classes of cottonwood trees. A closer inspection of the channels revealed that they contain good populations of cattail, rush species, bulrush, coyote willow, Gooding willow, and some tamarisk. The channels are aggrading and the riparian areas are expanding.

Vegetation conditions in the foreground appear to be little changed since Jackson photographed this site. Greasewood, big sagebrush, shadscale, and snakeweed are still present. Cheatgrass and the two juniper plants at the left of the scene are new. The ruins, including the "series of large stones set upon end and projecting 5-7 feet above the surface" noted by Jackson, have not significantly changed since 1875.

22

Photo 7a.

Photo 7b.

8. Utah/Arizona State Line Near Littlefield, Arizona

These photos were taken immediately adjacent to mile post No. 13 on the Utah/ Arizona State line, 13 miles east of the Arizona/Nevada/Utah tricorner monument. The original photo (8a) was taken March 13, 1901 (Carpenter, chief of survey party). It was retaken on March 30, 1993 (Hindley, BLM). The view is to the west; Arizona is to the left and Utah is to the right.

The 1901 photo is a typical example of how the original photographer wanted to demonstrate the difficulties of the survey line he was "running" rather than the ambient vegetation and soil surface conditions. In addition, the photo is overexposed, which decreases its value for comparison. However, it is of some value because vegetation "types" can be determined and compared to a current image.

There appears to be little, if any, change in plant density or distribution between the photos. There may be a slight decrease in curlygrass with a corresponding increase in annuals (red brome and cheatgrass). Creosote plants occupy the same locations as they did in 1901. The small stand of joshua plants is evident in the lower left corner of both photos. A still-usable Civilian Conservation Corps water tank is located approximately ½ mile southeast of where the photos were taken.

9. The White Cliffs Near Bryce Canyon National Park, Utah

The view in these photos is to the east-southeast toward Deer Spring Point, which is visible in the background (NW¼ SE¼ sec. 19, T. 40 S., R. 4 W.). The original photo (9a) was taken in 1921 (Moore, USGS). It was retaken (9b) on April 20, 1993 (Sintz, BLM), approximately 100 feet west and uphill from the original because juniper trees now block the view from where the 1921 photo was taken.

The pinyon-juniper community has obviously replaced the sagebrush-grass community that dominated the original scene. Young juniper and possibly pinyon trees can be seen in the foreground in the 1921 image. Encroachment of the pinyon-juniper stand from the slopes to the valley is obvious from the stairstepping age classes.

The cause and effect relationship of the pinyon-juniper encroachment throughout the Great Basin and Colorado Plateau is still being debated. Betancourt (1987) reports that the debate about the relative influences of livestock, fire suppression, and climate in the most recent pinyon-juniper invasion parallels the controversy over what caused historic arroyo cutting. Neilson (1987) indicates that overgrazing alone is not enough to cause pinyon-juniper expansion and natural fire might hinder pinyon-juniper seedling establishment. There is a growing number of observers (Mehringer and Wigand, 1987 and Davis, 1987) who report that the current pinyon-juniper invasion in the Great Basin and the Colorado Plateau is a cyclic phenomenon that has been occurring over the last 2,000 to 4,000 years. These findings were based on radiocarbon-dated pollen studies of packrat and woodrat middens and lake sediments in the Southwest and Great Basin. Mihringer and Wigland (1987) further state that these cycles occur when precipitation is plentiful.

Photo 8a.

Photo 8b.

Photo 9a.

Photo 9b.

26

Additional research will be required to support or modify these judgments. What is clear is that there is an emerging concept that so-called pristine vegetative conditions were not as romantically perceived. Stolzenburg (1994) states, "Classical notions of nature are under renovation. With archaic clues and modern tools, scientists are burying old balance-of-nature stereotypes, and uncovering a surprisingly dynamic past, punctuated with rapid turnovers of fauna and flora."

10. Salt Desert Shrub Site Near Moab, Utah

These photos were taken approximately 20 miles northwest of Moab, Utah (SW 1/4 sec. 12, T. 23 S., R. 19 E.). The view is to the northeast, toward Little Valley. The original photo (10a) was taken around 1940 (Smith, Utah State University). It was retaken (10b) on August 2, 1994 (Hindley, BLM).

The point where the photos were taken is now within the right-of-way for State Route No. 163. When the original photograph was taken, the highway was located approximately 1/4 mile west of its present position. The railroad track, which is visible slightly above the center of the photos, was built to serve the Moab potash plant in the early 1960's.

There has been an apparent increase in plant density and composition between 1940 and 1994. The only plant species visible in the 1940 photo appear to be shadscale and a few curlygrass plants. Plant species in the 1994 photo include shadscale, curlygrass, Indian ricegrass, sand dropseed, and cheatgrass. Vegetation conditions outside the right-of-way are the same as those within the fence line.

11. Book Cliffs Near Crescent Junction, Utah

The view in these photos is looking northeast toward Floy Canyon (NW 1/4 SE 1/4 sec. 4, T. 23 S., R. 18 E.). The original photo (11a) was taken in 1909 (Richardson, USGS). It was retaken (11b) on August 5, 1994 (Hindley, BLM).

The 1909 photo's lack of clarity makes close comparison difficult. However, it does appear that overall plant density has increased, with grass species having increased in both density and percent composition. Current vegetation includes Indian ricegrass, curlygrass, shadscale, and matt saltbush, with some cheatgrass and snakeweed.

Photo 10a.

Photo 10b.

Photo 11a.

Photo 11b.

Literature Cited

Betancourt, J.L. 1987. Paleoecology of Pinyon-Juniper Woodlands: Summary. USDA Forest Service Technical Report INT-215, pp. 129-139.

Davis, O.K. 1987. Palynological Evidence for Historic Juniper Invasion in Central Arizona: A Late-Quaternary Perspective. USDA Forest Service Technical Report INT-215, pp. 120-124.

Graf, W.L. 1978. Fluvial Adjustments to the Spread of Tamarisk in the Colorado Plateau Region. Geological Society of America Bulletin, V. 89, No. 10, pp. 1491-1501.

Gregory, H.E. 1950. Geology and Geography of the Zion Park Region, Utah and Arizona. U.S. Geological Survey Professional Paper 220, 200 pp.

Johnson, K.L. 1987. Rangeland Through Time: A Photographic Study of Vegetation Change in Wyoming, 1870-1976, Misc. Pub. 50 Agriculture Experiment Station University of Wyoming, 188 pp.

Klett, M., E. Manchester, J. Verberg, G. Bushaw, and R. Dingus. 1984. Second View: The Rephotographic Survey Project. University of New Mexico Press, 224 pp.

Linhart, S.M. 1993. An Historical Perspective of Change in Riparian Vegetation Along the Virgin River. Master's Thesis, University of Colorado, Denver, Colorado, 79 pp.

Mason, L. 1963. Using Historical Records To Determine Climax Vegetation. Journal of Soil and Water Conservation 18 (5):190-194.

Mehringer, P.J. and P.E. Wigand. 1987. Western Juniper in the Holocene. USDA Forest Service Technical Report INT-215, pp. 109-119.

Neilson, R.P. 1987. On the Interface Between Current Biological Studies and the Paleobotany of Pinyon-Juniper Woodlands. USDA Forest Service Technical Report INT-215, pp. 93-98.

Rogers, G.F. 1982. Then and Now: A Photographic History of Vegetation Change in the Central Great Basin Desert. University of Utah Press, Salt Lake City, Utah, 152 pp.

_____, H.E. Malde, and R.M. Turner. 1984. Bibliography of Repeat Photography for Evaluating Landscape Change. University of Utah Press, Salt Lake City, Utah, 179 pp.

Stephens, H.G. and E.M. Shoemaker. 1987. In The Footsteps of John Wesley Powell. Johnson Books, Boulder, Colorado, 286 pp.

Stolzenburg, W. 1994. New Views of Ancient Times. Nature Conservancy, September/October, pp. 10-15.

Veatch, F.M. 1969. Analysis of a 24-Year Photographic Record of Nisqualy Glacier, Mount Rainier National Park, Washington. U.S. Geological Survey Paper 631, 52 pp.

Webb, R.H., S.S. Smith, and V.A.S. McCord. 1991. Historic Channel Change of Kanab Creek. Grand Canyon Natural History Association. Monograph No. 9, 52 pp.

U.S. GPO J-777-180 11/96

REPORT DOCUMENTATION PAGE

Form Approved
OMB No. 0704-0188

Public reporting burden for this collection of information is estimated to average 1 hour per response, including the time for reviewing instructions, searching existing data sources, gathering and maintaining the data needed, and completing and reviewing the collection of information. Send comments regarding this burden estimate or any other aspect of this collection of information, including suggestions for reducing this burden, to Washington Headquarters Services, Directorate for Information Operations and Reports, 1215 Jefferson Davis Highway, Suite 1204, Arlington, VA 22202-4302, and to the Office of Management and Budget, Paperwork Reduction Project (0704-0188), Washington, DC 20503.

1. AGENCY USE ONLY *(Leave blank)*	2. REPORT DATE	3. REPORT TYPE AND DATES COVERED
	September 1996	Final

4. TITLE AND SUBTITLE

RIPARIAN AREA MANAGEMENT TR 1737-13
Observing Physical and Biological Change Through Historical Photographs

5. FUNDING NUMBERS

6. AUTHOR(S)

Earl Hindley

7. PERFORMING ORGANIZATION NAME(S) AND ADDRESS(ES)

U.S. Department of the Interior
Bureau of Land Management - National Applied Resource Sciences Center
P.O. Box 25047
Denver, CO 80225-0047

8. PERFORMING ORGANIZATION REPORT NUMBER

BLM/RS/ST-96/008+1737

9. SPONSORING/MONITORING AGENCY NAME(S) AND ADDRESS(ES)

10. SPONSORING/MONITORING AGENCY REPORT NUMBER

11. SUPPLEMENTARY NOTES

12a. DISTRIBUTION/AVAILABILITY STATEMENT

12b. DISTRIBUTION CODE

13. ABSTRACT *(Maximum 200 words)*

This technical reference provides an approach for using historical photos to analyze vegetation and stream channel conditions and trends for riparian-wetland areas.

14. SUBJECT TERMS

- Wetlands
- Riparian areas
- Vegetation
- Historic Photographs

15. NUMBER OF PAGES

36 including covers

16. PRICE CODE

17. SECURITY CLASSIFICATION OF REPORT	18. SECURITY CLASSIFICATION OF THIS PAGE	19. SECURITY CLASSIFICATION OF ABSTRACT	20. LIMITATION OF ABSTRACT
Unclassified	Unclassified	Unclassified	UL

Standard Form 298 (Rev. 2-89)
Prescribed by ANSI Std. Z39-18
298-102